Wharfedale

A Visitor's Guide
by Ron and Lucie Hinson

illustrated by Tom Sykes

DALESMAN BOOKS
1980

THE DALESMAN PUBLISHING COMPANY LTD.
CLAPHAM (via Lancaster), NORTH YORKSHIRE

First published (in this format) 1980

© Text, Ron and Lucie Hinson, 1958, 1980

© Illustrations, Tom Sykes, 1980

ISBN: 0 85206 607 4

Printed in Great Britain by
GEORGE TODD & SON
Marlborough Street, Whitehaven

Contents

An Introduction	5
Langstrothdale	9
Buckden to Kettlewell	13
Kilnsey and Littondale	16
Around Grassington	19
Burnsall to Barden	23
Down Dale	27

Map by E. Jeffrey

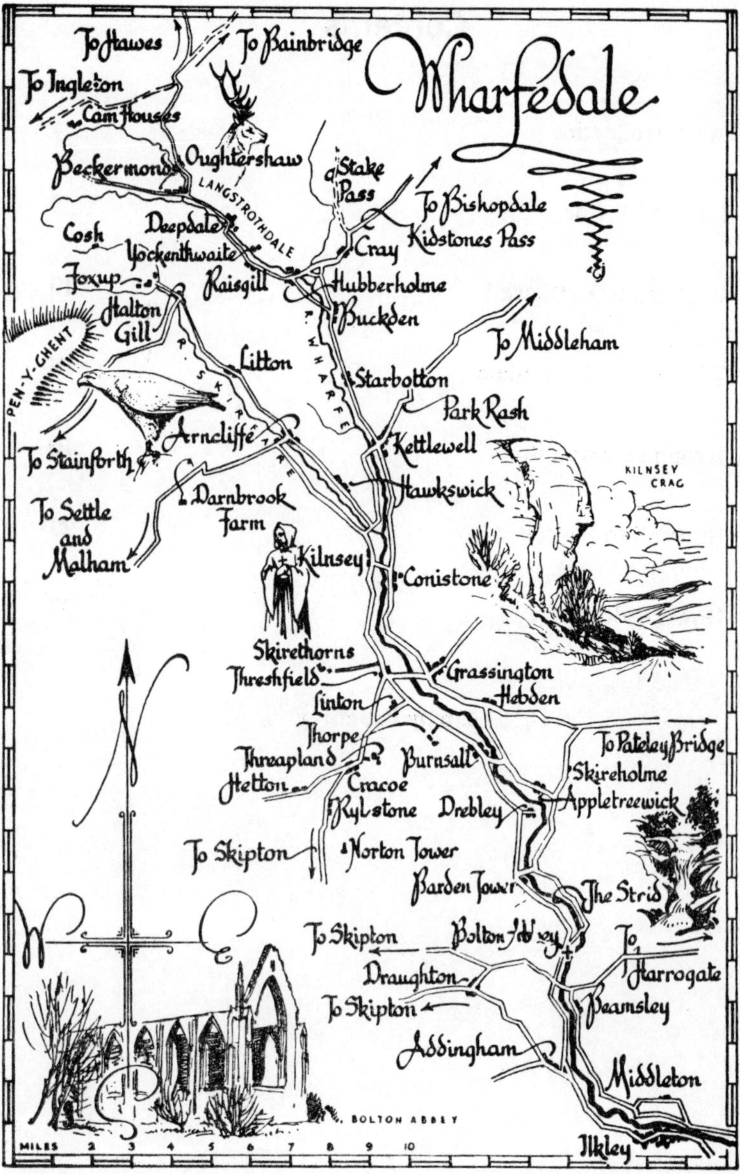
Wharfedale
To Hawes
To Bainbridge
To Ingleton
Cam Houses
Beckermonds
Oughtershaw
LANGSTROTHDALE
Stake Pass
To Bishopdale
Kidstones Pass
Deepdale
Cosh
Yockenthwaite
Cray
Foxup
Raisgill
Hubberholme
Halton Gill
PEN-Y-GHENT
Buckden
To Middleham
R. SKIRFARE
R. WHARFE
Litton
Starbotton
Park Rash
Arncliffe
Kettlewell
To Stainforth
KILNSEY CRAG
Darnbrook Farm
Hawkswick
To Settle and Malham
Kilnsey
Conistone
Skirethorns
Threshfield
Grassington
Linton
Hebden
Thorpe
To Pateley Bridge
Threapland
Burnsall
Skireholme
Hetton
Cracoe
Rylstone
Drebley
Appletreewick
To Skipton
Norton Tower
Barden Tower
The Strid
To Skipton
Bolton Abbey
To Harrogate
Draughton
Beamsley
To Skipton
Addingham
Middleton
BOLTON ABBEY
MILES 2 3 4 5 6 7 8 9 10
Ilkley

An Introduction

THIS is an introduction to Wharfedale, from the high fells at the head of Langstrothdale, where the main feeder streams of the Wharfe have their source, to the old bridge at Ilkley, under which the river swirls on its way to join the Ouse at Cawood. These words and pictures will do no more than introduce you to the valley, for the scenery of Wharfedale is more diverse than any of the other great Yorkshire dales and cannot be taken in at a glance. Human endeavour began when skin-clad men caught fish in lakes left by the glacier, and down the centuries which followed the Wharfedale story has been flavoured by Romans, Norman lords, the cowled monks of great abbeys, by farmers, craftsmen and lead-miners. There is an almost bewildering variety of strange stories and ancient traditions.

Early man was comparatively numerous. The remains of his habitations lie on the western fells of Littondale, and near Yockenthwaite, Grassington, Skirethorns, Thorpe, Appletreewick and Ilkley. The Romans had a town at Ilkley which was named Olicana. They mined the lead on the high fells around Greenhow, and they drove roads through the difficult country. Invasions of Angles and Saxons, Danes and Norsemen, helped to mould the dale's present life.

With the coming of the Normans, the rough grass, scrub and woodland which covered a large part of Wharfedale was enclosed for hunting. The monks of Fountains and Bolton superimposed sheep farming on a vast scale, and they also mined lead and milled corn. The pillaging Scots disturbed the peace of Wharfedale during this period of the Middle Ages, sparing neither monk nor peasant. When the Scotsmen were about, hidden Thorpe was a place at which women, children and cattle were safely concealed.

The important Lords of the Manor were, firstly Saxon Earl Edwin of Mercia. He was killed after clashes with Norman William, and his Wharfedale lands passed to Robert Romille, a Norman lord. It was Robert's granddaughter who gave the site at Bolton to the Augustinian canons of Embsay, and she gave Kilnsey to the Cistercians of Fountains Abbey. After the Romille line had ended, the Honour of Skipton passed to the Cliffords. Henry, the Shepherd Lord Clifford, led his dalesmen tenants to the Battle of Flodden, which brought to an end the period of Scottish nuisance. The men of Craven were to play a significant part in the battle, for they counter-attacked when the English Army started to give way after hours of fighting. A possible defeat was turned into an overwhelming victory.

The land held by the monasteries was sold when Henry VIII dissolved these great religious houses. Some of the land was bought by the people. The Cliffords purchased Bolton. The Yorkes, of Gouthwaite, in Nidderdale, came to own Appletreewick and Kilnsey. In the seventeenth century a feud raged between the Cliffords and the Yorkes, some of whom lived at Parcevall Hall, near Appletreewick. Lady Anne Clifford, last of the Cliffords, became a legend in the valley and was almost 'Queen' of the Dales, having large possessions in both Craven and Westmorland. She rebuilt the old hunting lodge at Barden, which had lain in ruins for many years. A Clifford married an Earl of Cork and Burlington, and the descendants were responsible for the fanciful buildings around Bolton. A descendant of this line married a Duke of Devonshire, with whose family the property still remains.

In the eighteenth century, hand-knitting was added to the domestic weaving, lead-mining, corn-milling and sheep-shearing which were the main industries of the valley, and the Shorthorn cow was being developed in the Dales country. One bred at Bolton Abbey weighed 312st. 8lb. It was exhibited at places all over the country. Apart from spasmodic revivals, lead-mining ended last century, and home-weaving too, passed out of Wharfedale's life. Today, the main industries are farming, the quarrying of limestone, and tourism.

Oughtershaw, a hamlet at the head of Langstrothdale.

Hubberholme bridge and church.

Langstrothdale

WHARFE is a swift, clear river which has its source with the merger of two mountain streams at Beckermonds (the name Beckermonds signifies 'the mouth of the becks'). For the source of the main feeder stream you must tramp on to Cam Fell, where an old Roman road runs between the fort at Bainbridge and Ingleton, passing close to a remote cluster of buildings, Cam Houses. Cam, incidentally, means 'a ridge of hills.' Where the Oughtershaw and Greenfield Becks merge at Beckermonds, the Wharfe is born.

From Beckermonds, at 1,000 feet above sea level, to Hubberholme, at 800 feet, the infant Wharfe flows through Langstrothdale, which in Norman times was preserved as a hunting ground. Until the reign of Henry VIII the manorial rights rested with the Percys, and they descended through marriage to the Cliffords. In 1241, William de Percy had seven lodges for his foresters. Henry de Percy, who fell at Bannockburn, was supervisor and chief warden of the chase of Langstrothdale and Littondale.

In this steep-sided valley the Wharfe shows itself at its best, cutting through limestone, forming fascinating pools and small waterfalls. Here you find the little hamlet of Deepdale. Yockenthwaite, reached by way of a tall bridge, originally meant 'Eogan's clearing.' Near Deepdale is an ancient stone circle. The Beresfords, a well-known local family, have lived in the dale for almost 300 years. Their ancestors came to Yorkshire from Hampshire to mine lead in the seventeenth century.

Hubberholme, named after a Viking chieftain, has a church which is an architectural gem. It was built before either Fountains or Bolton Abbeys, being intended as a chapel-of-ease to St. Oswald's, at Arncliffe, which lies over the fell, in Littondale. Hubberholme was served for many years by the curate of Halton Gill, at the head of Littondale — another chapel-of-ease to Arncliffe — and the minister had hard and difficult journeys over the Horse Head Pass, which rises to almost 2,000 feet above sea level. Now Hubberholme has a resident vicar. Hubberholme church, squat and grey, is full of character, both inside and out. The interior has rough-cut stone piers and walls. Iron candelabra were retained, although electricity has now been installed. A beautiful oak rood loft is one of few remaining in England. It used to hold the rood, or crucifix. The fine modern pews and choir stalls were made by Thompson, the 'mouse-man' of Kilburn.

Across the bridge from Hubberholme church, by the side of the main road, stands the *George Inn,* which until recently was the property of the Benefice. At one time it was the home of the parson. Here, on New Year's Day, the Hubberholme 'Parliament' meets. Local farmers bid for the tenancy of a sixteen-acre field on Kirkgill Pasture, which was left in trust for the benefit of the parish poor, and the rent paid is usually about £35. The vicar auctions the land on behalf of the church, and he and his two churchwardens officiate from the dining room, which is the 'House of Lords.' The company, mainly farmers, gathers in the small parlour of the inn, and comprises the 'House of Commons.' Nowadays there are no poor in the original sense, and the money goes to help the old-age pensioners. The vicarage at Hubberholme was built as a memorial to Bishop Reginald Heber and his family.

The White Lion at Cray.

Starbotton, a pleasant village built round a winding road.

Buckden to Kettlewell

STANDING on the lower slopes of the Pike (2,302 feet), Buckden lies nineteen miles from Skipton, the market town. It derives its names from the presence of deer, and within living memory a small herd was maintained here by Miss Compton Stansfield. After Miss Stansfield's death, the deer were disposed of, and the last of them was shot by a local farmer, Frank Horner. The antler from this animal may be seen at the *White Lion Inn,* at Cray, near Buckden. Cray lies at the bottom of the Kidstones Pass, which leads into Bishopdale and also, by the way, into the old North Riding. Buckden housed the foresters in Norman times, when Langstrothdale was a chase for wild animals. It lies astride a Roman road running from Ilkley to Bainbridge, and there is a grand walk along the section north of the village. It runs on the flanks of Buckden Pike.

Downdale from Buckden lies Starbotton, and the village largely dates from the seventeenth century, for in June, 1686, there was a disastrous flood, which swept away land and buildings. Damage at Starbotton was estimated at £3,000 and Kettlewell was badly affected as well. Starbotton is now a pleasant village built around a winding road, which takes the traveller over a narrow bridge crossing the once so angry beck. The Wharfe is a quarter of a mile away to the west.

Kettlewell was a busy place when the Domesday Book was being compiled. Its prosperity continued, for three abbeys—Coverham, Fountains and Bolton—had possessions here. There were highly productive lead mines on the moors, but they are now disused. The Manor of Kettlewell is governed by Trust Lords. In 1605 it became the property of the Crown by the attainder of the Nevilles. They lived at Middleham Castle, in Wensleydale. Then the manor came into the possession of a group of London merchants, who sold it to eight Kettlewell men in 1656. The Trust Lords draw rent from land and use this money for filling in shafts, repairing the moor gates, and for other repairs. Kettlewell lost some of its commercial importance when the Wharfedale railway was built only as far as Grassington. A small Norman church was rebuilt at the beginning of last century, but the tub-shaped font dates from Norman times. C. J. Cutcliffe Hyne, the novelist, lived at Kettlewell. He once advocated a watercress industry for the Dales, and went panning for gold in the streams near the village. Cutcliffe Hyne had travelled to the remote parts of the world, but he loved Kettlewell and is buried in the local churchyard.

There is a fine walk from Kettlewell to the top of Great Whernside (2,310 feet), and this walk can be continued from the summit into the upper part of Nidderdale. Great Whernside is stinted for the purpose of sheep grazing. There are 999 gaits, each representing the pasturage of a sheep. Hag Dike, once a farm, and close to the summit of Great Whernside, has now been restored and fitted out as a field centre for scouting.

A green lane running on the fell behind the village was an old monks' road over to Coverham Abbey. On the fell top it is met by a track from Starbotton, and after about a mile and a half is joined by the metalled road which runs from Coverdale to Kettlewell, via Park Rash. Now fit for motor traffic, but prohibited to motor coaches, Park Rash was once a part of the coaching route from London to Richmond, via Skipton. The hill, with its S-bends, is still a nerve-racking experience for strangers, but the view of the steep-sided valley, with winding Park Gill in the bottom and distant Wharfedale beyond, is worth the effort. The name 'Park' came from a large enclosure hereabouts. It was made by the Nevilles, of Middleham, for hunting, and was named Scale Park. 'Rash' indicates a steep hill.

A mile south of Kettlewell is Scar Gill, a Church of England centre with a magnificent chapel set against a backcloth of pine trees.

The Racehorses and Bluebell at Kettlewell.

Kilnsey and Littondale

THOUSANDS of people know Kilnsey Crag, the grey, Sphinx-like cliff against which the Wharfedale glacier rubbed its shoulders during the last chapters of the Ice Age, and near which one of the most important of the Dales agricultural shows takes place each summer. The village of Kilnsey is no less deserving of attention. It originally formed part of the great Skipton estates. Then, in 1156, Alice de Romille (who founded Bolton Priory) gave Kilnsey to the monks of Fountains, and it became the most important grange in Craven. Wool from the flocks of Craven was exported to Italy and the Low Countries. When the monastery was dissolved, Kilnsey came to the Wade family. About a century later, Mr. Cuthbert Wade used the monastic building as a quarry for his new house—Kilnsey Hall—which lies at the head of this village's single street.

Although Kilnsey Crag is best viewed, perhaps, from Kilnsey itself, there is a splendid view from Conistone, on the opposite side of the valley, a village containing some fine seventeenth century houses.

Branching away from the main valley near Kilnsey is Littondale, Wordsworth's 'deep fork of Amerdale.' The valley is only one mile long, watered by the river Skirfare, which joins the Wharfe at Amerdale Dub, where the larger river passes through a breached moraine. This small, secluded dale was the home of many Iron Age men, whose habitations are scattered along the western fells. Sheep farming and hunting comprise the dale's main early history, for it had only one mill and very little lead-mining took place. The valley lay within the Percy Fee, and Richard de Percy presented it to Fountains Abbey, who grazed sheep here. The monks had a grange at Arncliffe. Although the valley is named after Litton, the main village is Arncliffe, where most of the houses cluster round a green. The name refers to the nesting of eagles. Near the river stands Arncliffe church, which is of Norman foundation, and is the mother church of Halton Gill and Hubberholme. The church was rebuilt except for the tower, in 1796, and was

further restored in 1841. An old house near the bridge—
'Bridge End'—was once owned by the Hammond family,
who built Amerdale House. While staying with Walter Morrison, of Malham Tarn House, the Rev. Charles Kingsley
was introduced to the Hammonds, and enjoyed the hospitality of one of the family at 'Bridge End.' The river, the
house, and the lady herself were incorporated in the early
chapters of his classic children's book, *The Water Babies*.
This little valley is the Vendale of the book.

From the valley slopes you can look down the dale and
see the effects of glacial action. Limestone walls form
intricate patterns on the floor of the valley, and they range
boldly over the fells. Monks in early times built a few
enclosing walls, and in the sixteenth century some walls
were built on the outlying moors so that sheep could be prevented from straying. At the same time farmers began to
enclose by stone walls the fields in the immediate vicinity
of their houses or village. The irregular and seemingly
senseless shapes of fields stems from this period. More, and
still irregular, enclosing was done in the next century or
so, but it was the Enclosure Acts of the late 1700s that
began the great wall-building era. Long, straight and good
walls, they enclosed the common land in rectangles.

Arncliffe bridge and church.

A fold at Linton, one of the most attractive villages in the Dales.

Around Grassington

BETWEEN Conistone and Grassington lies Grass Wood, which is botanically famous, for over 300 varieties of flowers grow here. Although the wood is private, public footpaths run through it, and visitors should not, of course, pick the flowers and thus lessen the wood's botanical importance. Grass Wood was purchased by a timber firm in 1955, but assurances were given that local amenities would be preserved. Part of the wood has been leased to the Yorkshire Naturalists' Union as a nature reserve and is wardened. It was in Grass Wood that Tom Lee, a young Grassington blacksmith, murdered Dr. Richard Petty, a medical practitioner, after a quarrel. Lee threw the body into the Wharfe from Loup Scar, between Grassington and Burnsall. Lee was brought to trial, and his body was gibbeted on the road between the two villages in 1768. Bastow Wood, a higher neighbour of Grass Wood, belongs to Linton Hospital, an almshouse for six old men or women. Above the wood, on Lea Green, are the remains of an Iron Age village and the fields attached to it.

Grassington is the largest and—commercially—most important village in Upper Wharfedale. It continues to grow at a speedy rate, and has a fine secondary modern school of contemporary design. Anglians founded Grassington during the sixth century A.D., but there are many traces round about of life in prehistoric times. Here you can find the remains of an old theatre that flourished for many years at the beginning of the 1800s. The leading spirit of the 'Grassington Thespians' was Thomas Airey (1771-1842), for many years the local postmaster and carrier. Edmund Kean acted at the theatre in 1807. Grassington's Square was recobbled to a high standard of craftsmanship in 1973.

Threshfield, across the river, was the rail head of the line from Skipton, which is now closed and dismantled beyond Swinden. Close to the former station is a Roman Catholic church in a controversial style of modern architecture. Threshfield itself has not suffered too badly from its close proximity to the lime quarries. Within living memory, John

Delaney, founder of the quarry, also mined coal nearby. The school here was once haunted by 'Old Pam,' an impish little fellow. Lime quarrying on a large scale is quite a modern innovation, though for centuries the limestone was burned in small kilns for local use. Today only extraction and not burning takes place at Threshfield. The main industry in the Grassington area for centuries was lead-mining. On Grassington Moor, to the north-east of the village, you find the disused mines and ruined buildings. One shaft sunk on Grassington Moor was over a hundred fathoms deep. About 1854, the lead mines employed about 200 men and were producing from 700 to 900 tons of refined lead annually. One of the factors leading to their closure was the importation of cheaper foreign lead. The smelt mill chimney has been preserved.

Grassington Bridge (1604) is the oldest existing bridge over the upper Wharfe, though it has grown enormously. The original bridge was hump-backed, designed for pack-horses. It was later widened and flattened, as can be clearly seen if you look underneath at the Grassington end, and on the face of the bridge on the downstream side. Above the bridge, below Grass Wood, the water is tormented at the Ghaistrills, and there is an equally fine spectacle at Linton Falls, where the line of the Craven Fault can be seen. From the bank of the Wharfe there is a splendid view of Linton church, of Transitional and Decorated Gothic architecture, with a Norman font. Until about ninety years ago, the parish was in two ecclesiastical halves. Linton thereby had two rectors, who lived in houses which adjoined—and took the services alternately! When the river is low, stepping stones can be used to cross the water.

Linton is one of the most attractive villages in the Dales, a claim which was supported by a newspaper campaign aimed at finding the loveliest village. Linton was adjudged the winner, and a sundial was presented to commemorate the fact. It stands on the green in front of Linton 'Hospital,' almshouses given by a native of the village, Richard Fountain, who found fame and fortune in London, becoming an alderman of the city. He died in 1721. The beck at Linton is crossed by three bridges and a ford, which are all close together. Halliwell Sutcliffe, author of *The Striding Dales*

The Square and Main Street, Grassington.

and many other Dales books, lived at White Abbey, Linton, and the village is the home of Dr. Arthur Raistrick, a great authority on Dales history, traditions and industry.

Around Grassington there is an almost bewildering number of roads. Strangers might be pardoned for thinking they should have carried a compass on their journeys! From Grassington a road leads through Hebden to the heights of Greenhow, where lead was mined in a tongue of limestone from the times of the Romans to the early part of this century. Another road leads to Burnsall, following the line of the river. And there is a road which is joined by travelling through either Linton or Threshfield. It is an important route to Skipton, in Airedale. Skipton, indeed, is the market town for Upper Wharfedale. A section of this road to Skipton has been disfigured by lime quarrying.

By turning off the road to the left after passing the quarry, you can visit the hidden village of Thorpe. There are fairy associations with Elbolton, a cave near Thorpe, but much more important were discoveries of signs of Early

Man and ancient animals. The main road passes Threapland, Cracoe and Rylstone, or you may branch away to the right beyond Cracoe and journey through Hetton to Gargrave. Threapland today consists of a single farm, but there was a time when other buildings stood hereabouts, including a mill for the grinding of corn. Wharfedale is left behind at Cracoe, limit of the watershed.

At Rylstone you can see a village green that was flooded. During the nineteenth century it was succeeded by a pond. Rylstone church was rebuilt during the same century. Behind the church stood Rylstone Hall, home of the Nortons, who fared badly during the Pilgrimage of Grace, and their experiences are recounted by Wordsworth in *The White Doe of Rylstone*. On the slopes of Rylstone Fell are the remnants of a tower built by the Nortons to protect their rights against their bitter enemies, the Cliffords of Skipton. According to the Rev. B. J. Harker, Rylstone Cross was put up to commemorate the Battle of Waterloo.

The classic view of Burnsall from the road down dale.

Burnsall to Barden

RETURNING to the Wharfe valley at Burnsall, the traveller finds a present-day tourist centre by the river, with a broad green on which a maypole stands. Burnsall Sports have been held on 'the first Saturday after the first Sunday after the twelfth of August' since the days of the first Elizabeth, and a fell race was inaugurated about 1850. Burnsall is actually of very old foundation, and many pre-Norman pieces are to be found in and around the church. There are stocks in the churchyard, which is entered by an unusual lychgate.

The chief glory of Burnsall is the river, and the bridge which crosses it is the successor of many battered and flood-tormented bridges. The present structure dates from the 1880s. When Burnsall Bridge was restored in 1612 the bill was met by Sir William Craven—the 'Dick Whittington of the Dales.' Since he was born in a poor home at Appletreewick, he journeyed to London to seek his fortune, and eventually became Lord Mayor of the City. Sir William also rebuilt the church (1612) and endowed Burnsall Grammar School (1602). When the church was further restored in 1859, it suffered a great deal, losing its original chancel arch and its battlements.

There was a time when stories of fairies and ghosts were firmly believed by the folk of Wharfedale, and they also lived in fear of a spectral hound, with eyes as big as saucers—the barguest. This beast was said to have its lair in Trollers Gill, near Appletreewick. The gill, a fine limestone gorge about half a mile long, lies near Parcevall Hall. A footpath lies through a gate near a small bridge which bears a 'Private Road' notice, and you reach the gill in about fifteen minutes. There is no right of way through the gorge itself. Trolls were the little men of the mountains in Scandinavian folk-lore, and they were said to be very mischievous. The area must have once been a very evil locality, for less than two miles from Trollers Gill is Dibbles Bridge, which is said to have been built by the Devil. Parcevall Hall, the lovely gardens of which are open to the public in summer, was in existence in 1535. The Yorkes of Gouthwaite bought it a few years later, and William Nevison, the highwayman, is said to have used it as a hide-out. At one period it was a farmhouse. Restored with care by the late Sir William Milner, it is a beautiful Elizabethan house, and from it there is a fine view of Simon's Seat. The house was opened as a Diocesan retreat and conference centre in 1963.

Appletreewick is of Danish origin, and it was mentioned in Domesday Book. There was a time when it was held by the Romilles. Then Bolton Abbey bought it, and the Yorkes came into possession after monastic times. Appletreewick had an unusual fair and feast, the charter being held from the days of the monks. Lead was mined on the fells, and when the lead trade failed last century the local economy suffered badly. There are three halls in this straggling village. Monks' Hall, which has been greatly rebuilt or restored, belonged at one time to Bolton Abbey. It was one of the granges. High Hall was built by the Craven family, descendants of Sir William Craven, who was born in 1549 in a cottage which is now a chapel-of-ease. Low Hall, restored in 1658 by a William Preston, had a ghost which was finally exorcised after many noisy hauntings.

The road from Appletreewick descends to river level at Barden Bridge, which was erected in the seventeenth century, flinging three high arches across the river. A terrific flood brought a bridge down in 1673 — most of the other Wharfedale bridges suffered at the same time — and it was 'repaired at the expense of the whole of the West Riding' in 1676. Barden Bridge was extensively repaired in 1955. One of the finest riverside walks in Yorkshire begins at Barden Bridge where there is a car park and picnic area and extends through Bolton Wood to Bolton Abbey. When Wharfedale was largely given over to hunting, there was a forest lodge at Barden, owned by the Cliffords. Barden Tower was enlarged by Henry Clifford, the Shepherd Lord, in 1485. It fell into disuse until Lady Anne Clifford restored it in 1658. It had been ruined since about 1589. Later, after a period of neglect, its roof was taken off (in 1774), and the Tower fell into ruin once again. Camden said that at 'Barden-Towne' was 'a little turret belonging to the Earle of Cumberland, where there is round about good store of game and hunting of fat deere.' A road near Barden Tower leads over the moors to Embsay and Skipton.

Monks' Hall, Appletreewick.

Trollers Gill, near Appletreewick.

Barden Tower, restored by Lady Anne Clifford in 1658.

Down Dale

THOSE who walk by the river from Barden to Bolton eventually reach a point where the Wharfe, in the early manhood of its life, is angered by a channel of massive gritstone rocks. It stretches for nearly a quarter of a mile, forming a fantastic channel. This point is called The Strid, from *stryth,* a tumultuous rush of water. Motorists will see the approaches to The Strid signposted on the left of the road. Although The Strid is only a few feet wide, its depth extends to thirty or more feet, and the rocks are worn into cave-like hollows. A long pointed rock slopes down from the bank at the narrowest point, smoothed by the passage of human feet. This is the notorious Strid Jump, but the majority of the people who stand here have more regard for their safety than to attempt the crossing.

The leap required is not unusually long, but the bank is so formed that on landing the athlete can easily lose balance and fall or slip backwards. Such an accident is almost certain to be fatal, as the current will drag the luckless person into the deep undercut recess of the channel. Rock formations below the surface produce a pump-like suction. Mr. Christopher Bailey, of Keighley, used a ladder to explore The Strid in 1894. He stayed at a depth of twenty-five feet for nearly three minutes, and saw tree trunks bleached almost white, jammed in ledges of rock.

It was an accident here half-way through the twelfth century which is said to have resulted in the establishment of the Priory at Bolton. The word 'Priory' is used in connection with Bolton for the first time here, for although most people refer to it as Bolton Abbey, and this is the correct Post Office name, it was a Priory that was established near the Wharfe. The fatal accident happened to the Boy of Egremond, son of Alec de Romille, who was very fond of hunting. One day, with a greyhound at leash, he strode through the woods at a point near The Strid. He leapt across the foaming waters, as he had probably done many times before, but this day his dog held back, and he was drawn into the river and drowned. His mother was heartbroken, and some have declared that the Priory by the banks of the Wharfe was a memorial to the dead boy. Although he may indeed have been drowned at The Strid, the Priory was already established, for his signature is found on the title deeds! The Strid Wood Nature Trail, opened in 1973, provides a number of routes between The Strid and Bolton Priory.

The date of the founding of Bolton Priory was 1154, and the Augustinian canons came to the Wharfe valley from a breezier home at Embsay, near Skipton. While never considered a large establishment, Bolton numbered about 200 people including lay servants. Sheep were reared, and there was a sizeable trade in wool; the estates were industriously developed, and lead was mined. The Scots, the ever present menace from the beginning of the fourteenth century, robbed and pillaged the Priory several times until, eventually, a number of 'armed gentlemen' were kept for its defence.

The local people had used the nave of the Priory as a parish church, and they were given permission to continue to do so after the Dissolution. The west tower was being built at this time. It would have hidden a fine Early English West Front, but had the tower been completed this same front was to have come down. The Duke of Devonshire's shooting lodge was built onto the old gatehouse, and nearby is an eighteenth century archway spanning the road. It was an aqueduct for the mill. From the corner near the ornamental fountain, one of the fine views of the Abbey is now obscured by the growth of trees. It was at Bolton Abbey that the Rev. W. Carr bred the celebrated Craven Heifer, which weighed 312st. 8lb.

From the moor above Ilkley there are extensive views of Wharfedale. The National Park ends at Bolton Bridge. To the north-west is Beamsley Beacon, itself a fine vantage point. Beamsley village, out of sight from here—it lies a mile from Bolton Bridge—contains a 'hospital' or almshouses for old women. It was founded in 1593 by the mother of Lady Anne Clifford, and visitors may enter the chapel which is the centre of the circular building seen through the archway near the roadside. The seven tenants occupy seven little houses rent free, and enjoy a helpful bounty.

The Strid, highlight of the riverside walk from Barden to Bolton Abbey.

The Claphams were an important Beamsley family from the days of Edward III. They are said to have been buried upright in Bolton Priory.

Addingham, somewhat north of west in this view from Ilkley Moor, was the birthplace of that very industrious inventor, Samuel Cunliffe Lister, who lived to the age of ninety years, making a fortune from some of his 150 inventions. He became the first Baron Masham, the name being

The 18th century archway at Bolton Abbey.

taken from the locality of his estates in lower Wensleydale. Industry is very apparent in Addingham. It is a village of tall buildings, three-storey houses being the rule rather than the exception in the main street. They are a reminder of the days of domestic weaving.

The story of Ilkley's human associations leads back to the days of prehistory, for Ancient Man lived on the Moor. Here his earthworks, tumuli and stone circles are to be found. Ilkley's name is derived from the old word for rock — Ilacan. The connection between this name, the Roman name of Olicana, and the Domesday Book title of 'Illicleia' is apparent. This moorland settlement was one of the nine main towns of the Brigantes, who caused the Romans a great deal of trouble during the colonisation of the North. After the Romans left, their town in the valley was not important. It dwindled to a village, remaining so until (in 1843) the cult of hydropathy was introduced. Now it is a thriving town with many visitors. 'White Wells,' on the moor above the town, are two deep and circular old baths, hollowed out of rock and fed by an icy spring of pure and constant water.

A popular walk at Ilkley leads up to Heber's Gill on to the open moor, not far from the 'Swastika Stone,' a prehistoric rock carving of an ancient symbol of fire. In the town itself, the 'cup and ring stones' lie in an enclosure in Queen's Road. They were found on the Moor. The largest is about fifteen feet by twelve feet. How they originated is unknown, but similarly moulded stones have been found in various other parts of the world.

In the parish churchyard are the remains of three Saxon crosses. Two more lie in the church itself. There is some evidence in the form of altar stones that the church is a descendant of a Roman temple. The ground here was enclosed in the Roman fortress. Upstream from the road bridge, near a Roman ford, is a 200-year-old packhorse bridge, which motor traffic may no longer use.

Eastwards from Ilkley, the dale widens. The Wharfe, after flowing across the Vale of York, joins the Ouse near Cawood.

Bolton Bridge.

Cow and Calf Rocks, Ikley.